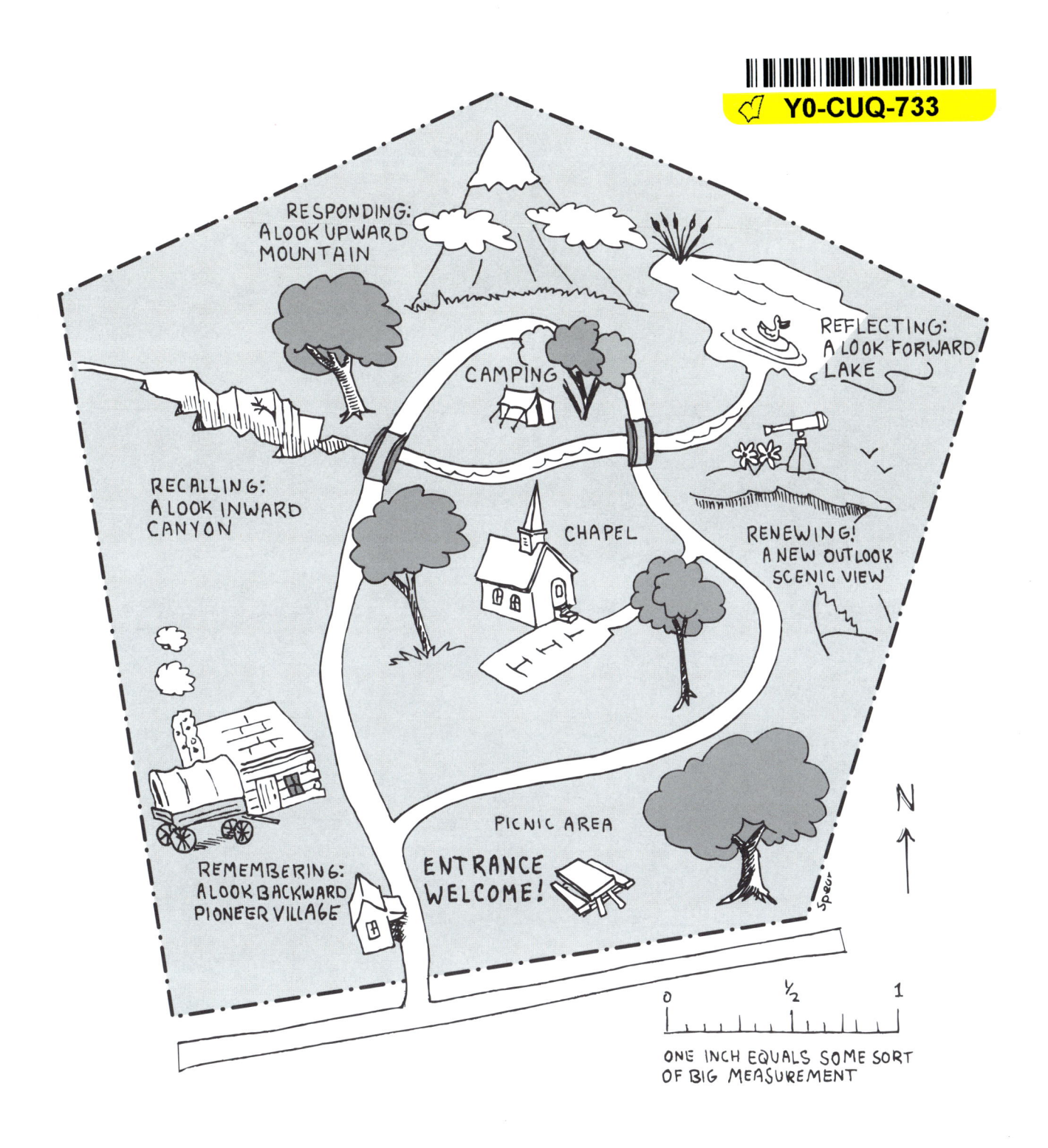

SPIRITUAL RETREAT

...A Weekend Alone With God

by Tom Armiger & Emily Sutherland

Copyright © 1995 by Wesleyan Publishing House
All Rights Reserved
Published by Wesleyan Publishing House
Indianapolis, Indiana 46250
Printed in the United States of America
ISBN 0-89827-139-8

Scripture taken from the HOLY BIBLE, NEW INTERNATIONAL VERSION®. NIV®. Copyright © 1973, 1978, 1984 by International Bible Society. Used by permission of Zondervan Publishing House. All rights reserved.

All rights reserved. No part of this publication may be reproduced, stored in a retrieval system, or transmitted in any form or by any means — electronic, mechanical, photocopy, recording or any other — except for brief quotations in printed reviews, without the prior written permission of the publisher.

Spiritual Retreat
...A Weekend Alone With God

INTRODUCTION

THE PURPOSE of this Spiritual Retreat is to take a time away from our busy lives to quietly focus on our friendship with God, our level of commitment and discipline for Him, and to give us a clearer picture of who He is and who we are.

THE KEY ELEMENTS of this weekend "journey" are:
- Prayer
- Solitude
- Spiritual Evaluation
- Confession
- Submission
- Bible Study and Meditation
- Listening
- Dreams and Goals
- Rejoicing and Celebration

THE MAIN OBJECTIVE of this Spiritual Retreat Weekend is to help us gain a fresh new passion for God and a clearer vision of what He wants from us.

THE PROGRAM FORMAT includes times of personal retreat mixed with times when everyone comes together for group sharing, prayer, and rejoicing together.

THE SESSION TOPICS ARE:
1. Remembering...A Look Backward
2. Recalling...A Look Inward
3. Responding...A Look Upward
4. Reflecting...A Look Forward
5. Renewing...A New Outlook

Spiritual Retreat

...A Weekend Alone With God

SAMPLE PROGRAM SCHEDULE

FRIDAY EVENING

7:00 - 8:30 p.m.	SESSION 1: REMEMBERING
8:30 - 9:30 p.m.	Group Rejoicing
9:30 - 11:00 p.m.	Group Relaxation
	Fellowship, food, and games

SATURDAY

8:00 - 8:30 a.m.	Breakfast
8:30 - 10:00 a.m.	SESSION 2: RECALLING
10:00 - Noon	SESSION 3: RESPONDING
Noon - 1:30 p.m.	Group Rejoicing
	Prayer & Fasting Time
1:30 - 2:00 p.m.	Group Relaxation Break
2:00 - 5:00 p.m.	SESSION 4: REFLECTING
	Solitude and Silence until supper
5:00 - 6:30 p.m.	Supper
7:00 - 9:00 p.m.	Group Rejoicing
	Reactions and Rewards of the Day
	Sharing Keepsake & Testimony
9:00 - 11:00 p.m.	Group Relaxation and Private Time

SUNDAY

8:00 - 8:30 a.m.	Breakfast
8:30 - 10:30 a.m.	SESSION 5: RENEWING
10:30 - 11:30 a.m.	Group Rejoicing
	Communion Service
Noon	Lunch and Depart

Spiritual Retreat
TOOLS FOR THE JOURNEY

Below is a list of spiritual disciplines and their definitions which are helpful in pursuing a strong relationship with God. Many of them will be used during this Weekend Alone With God.

STUDY OF THE WORD: Discovering things in God's Word that help you know more about Him, that give you wisdom in your everyday life, and that help you resist temptation to do wrong.

WORSHIP: Taking time to enjoy God's presence.

PRAYER: Any form of talking to God, whether silently, audibly, or even through writing.

SILENCE & SOLITUDE: Getting away from the noise of everyday life in order to be alone to think, meditate, pray, and/or listen to God.

MEMORIZATION: Studying and learning portions of God's Word so you can always have it in your heart as a constant reminder.

FASTING: Doing without something (usually food) for the purpose of prayer, meditation, and special time spent with God.

JOURNALING: Talking to God through writing, keeping written records of your relationship with Him, writing about special milestones in your life, and any other written messages you desire to keep.

MEDITATION: To concentrate on God's Word, allowing it to affect you more deeply than just hearing or reading, but actually letting it get into your heart.

SIMPLICITY & SACRIFICE: Doing without some of the "luxuries" of life for the purpose of relying more on God and focusing on the truly important things in life.

STEWARDSHIP: Giving back to God your time, your abilities, and your finances to show Him gratitude for all He has given you.

CONFESSION: Admitting to God your need for Him, sharing with Him specific things you have done, said, and thought that you are truly sorry for.

SUBMISSION: Allowing God to have control of your life and committing to following His will for your life.

GUIDANCE & ACCOUNTABILITY: Allowing God to use other people, along with His Word, to keep your focus on Him.

FELLOWSHIP & CELEBRATION: Sharing and listening to praises, lessons learned, and future dreams with others for the purpose of giving the glory and recognition to God.

PERSEVERANCE: Consistently pursuing an intimate relationship with God no matter who or what tries to hinder you!

WHAT GOD HAS DONE
WHAT GOD IS SAYING TO YOU NOW
GOD'S LEADERSHIP IN YOUR LIFE
YOUR COMMUNION WITH GOD

REMEMBERING
A Look Backward

> God also said to Moses, "Say to the Israelites, 'The LORD, the God of your fathers — the God of Abraham, the God of Isaac and the God of Jacob — has sent me to you.' **This is my name forever, the name by which I am to be remembered from generation to generation."**
>
> Exodus 3:15 (NIV)

Remembering what God has done in your past can be the means to discover what God wants to do in and through you in the future. The next few pages are to be used to record your spiritual journey up to right now.

Recording your spiritual journey is a great starting point to developing the spiritual discipline of journaling. Journaling is simply communicating with God via writing, and it can be a beneficial way to keep track of:

- What God has done

- What God is saying to you now

- God's leadership (past, present, and future) in your life in order to rejoice in His faithfulness and grace to you.

- Your communion with God through prayer, praise, and adoration.

FORMAT OPTIONS — Your spiritual journey record may take the style of an outline, a narrative, a map, a cartoon, or whatever means helps you to recount God's activity throughout your life.

ITEMS TO POSSIBLY INCLUDE — your family background, your childhood influences, your conversion, your mentors, and/or influences, crisis events, the mountaintop experiences, the valley encounters, your consecration to His Lordship, the struggles and challenges, the victories won, personal highlights and achievements, and personal failure or defeats.

REFLECT ON . . . How God has led you and kept you, your spiritual progress, lessons learned about yourself, lessons learned about God, weak areas recurring, stumbling blocks, or stepping stones.

MY SPIRITUAL HISTORY
Remembering What God Has Done

TURNING POINTS
Remembering key events that changed my direction

COUNTING MY BLESSINGS
List things about your past — and about the present — that you're thankful for!

"Your father's blessings are greater than the blessings of the ancient mountains, than the bounty of the age-old hills . . ."

Genesis 49:26

GOD'S ACTIVITY TOWARD ME

Remember how God has revealed himself to you, treated you, and/or protected you. What does this tell you about God?

A PRAYER OF ADORATION TO GOD

Dear God . . .

Amen

GROUP REJOICING

Worshiping and praising God together for who He is and what He has done!

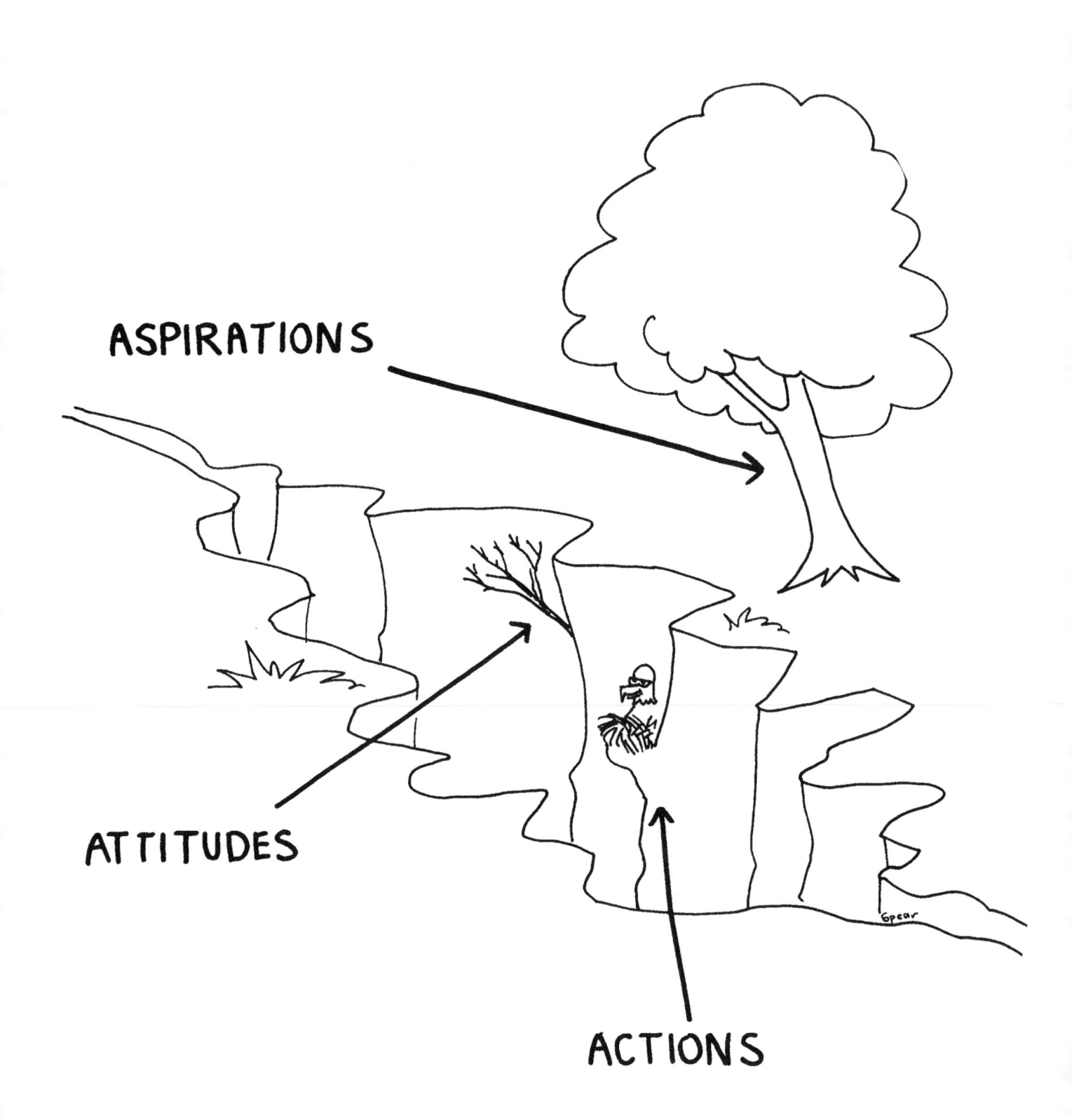

ASPIRATIONS

ATTITUDES

ACTIONS

RECALLING
A Look Inward

> **Therefore, if anyone is in Christ, he is a new creation; the old has gone, the new has come!**
>
> 2 Corinthians 5:17

In the last session you looked back at your history and thought about how God has fit into your life up to this point, but you are not the same person that you were before God was part of your life. Now you will have the opportunity to think about the person you really are inside and who you want to become.

What does God's Word reveal about you? You will have the opportunity to find that out very shortly. You will learn how God's Word fits into your:

1. Aspirations (Colossians 3:1-17)

2. Attitudes (Matthew 5:3-10)

3. Actions (James 1-5)

For each of these three areas you will read through the scripture given, then think about what you are like in comparison with what the verses say you can and should become. Don't just answer the questions, but think about what God's Word's says you need to work on.

At the end of this session, list the specific things you discovered that you need to work on in order to become the person God wants you to be.

MY LIFE ASPIRATIONS
Colossians 3:1-17

MY BIGGEST ASPIRATIONS

PUT OFF'S:

_____

_____

_____

_____

PUT ON'S:

_____

_____

_____

_____

I NEED TO BECOME . . .

THE RIGHT ATTITUDES
Matthew 5:3-10

Circle the number that best applies to you at the right of each "be-attitude":

1 = I believe this attitude is becoming evident in my life on a consistent basis.
2 = I am actively working on making this attitude a part of my daily life.
3 = I would like to have that attitude but I've got long way to go.
4 = I have never realized the need for this attribute and/or I have not taken the time to work on it at all.

1.	**A Humbled Heart**	1 2 3 4
2.	**A Broken Heart**	1 2 3 4
3.	**A Controlled Heart**	1 2 3 4
4.	**A Hungry Heart**	1 2 3 4
5.	**A Merciful Heart**	1 2 3 4
6.	**A Clean Heart**	1 2 3 4
7.	**A Peace-making Heart**	1 2 3 4
8.	**A Faithful Heart**	1 2 3 4

I NEED TO BECOME . . .

THE RIGHT ACTIONS
A STUDY ABOUT RIGHT ACTIONS

Instructions: Circle the numbers below that best indicate how often you give in to the actions listed in the left-hand column. The numbers are described as follows:

1 = *A lot.*
2 = *Sometimes.*
3 = *Hardly ever.*
4 = *Only under certain circumstances.* (What circumstances?)

1. Anger (James 1:20)	1 2 3 4
2. Untamed Tongue (James 1:26)	1 2 3 4
3. Showing Favoritism (James 2:1)	1 2 3 4
4. Critical (James 3:1)	1 2 3 4
5. Bragging (James 3:13)	1 2 3 4
6. Selfish ambition (James 3:14)	1 2 3 4
7. Envy (James 3:16)	1 2 3 4
8. Fighting (James 4:1)	1 2 3 4
9. Friendship with the world (James 4:4)	1 2 3 4
10. Loving the world (James 4:4)	1 2 3 4
11. Pride (James 4:6)	1 2 3 4
12. Slander against someone (James 4:11)	1 2 3 4
13. Knowing right, but not doing it (James 4:17)	1 2 3 4
14. Grumbling (James 5:9)	1 2 3 4
15. Swearing (James 5:12)	1 2 3 4

I NEED TO BECOME . . .

I NEED TO BECOME...

INSTRUCTIONS: Look back on the pages where you filled in the box "I need to become..." and list below the things that you wrote down which you need to work on so far.

- ❏ _____
- ❏ _____
- ❏ _____
- ❏ _____
- ❏ _____
- ❏ _____
- ❏ _____
- ❏ _____
- ❏ _____
- ❏ _____
- ❏ _____
- ❏ _____
- ❏ _____
- ❏ _____

List the top five in order of priority:

1.
2.
3.
4.
5.

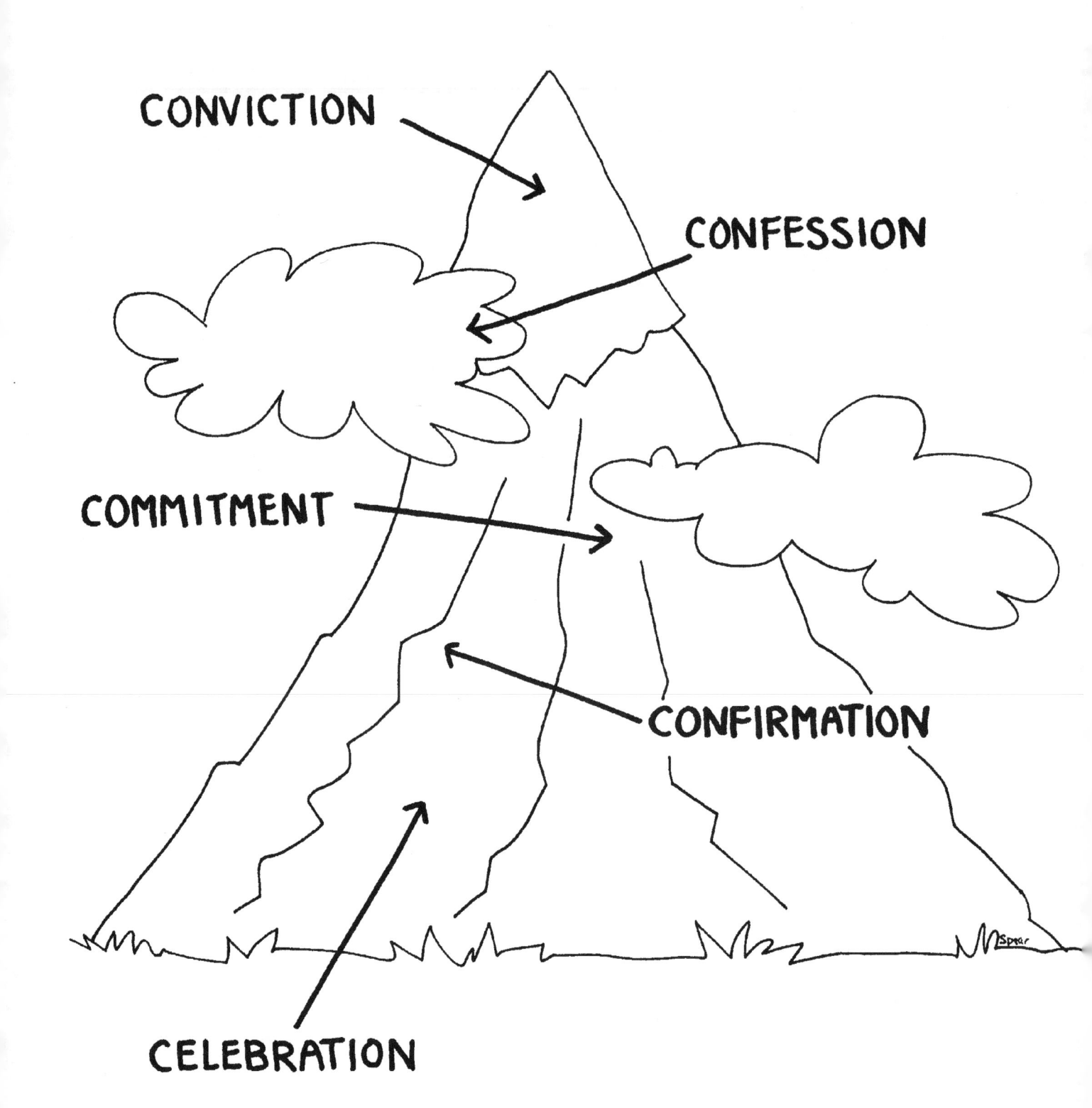

CONVICTION

CONFESSION

COMMITMENT

CONFIRMATION

CELEBRATION

RESPONDING
A Look Upward

During the next portion of this Weekend Alone With God you will be taking a walk through the five stages of spiritual life change listed below. You will take a prayer walk - outside if possible - stopping every few minutes to complete the five "stops" you will find on the following pages. Begin this walk by asking God to help you think clearly about what He is specifically saying to you.

Each stop represents one stage of the cycle that usually occurs during a life changing spiritual growth period. This cycle is called the "Cycle of Spiritual Life Change." The starting point can begin at any stage.

1. **CONVICTION**

2. **CONFESSION**

3. **COMMITMENT**

4. **CONFIRMATION**

5. **CELEBRATION**

Proceed by working on each "stop" of the cycle to begin your own spiritual life change.

STOP ONE
CONVICTION

God is calling me to change by putting off these things . . .

. . . and by putting on these things . . .

STOP TWO
CONFESSION

God has convicted me that I have displeased Him by ...

STOP THREE
COMMITMENT

In order to see God change me, I vow to be or do . . .

STOP FOUR
CONFIRMATION

God is empowering me to change by . . .

I will establish accountability for change with . . .

STOP FIVE
CELEBRATION

I'm praising God for victory in . . .

I will share what God has done with . . .

GROUP REJOICING TOGETHER
Worship, Praise & Testimonies

GROUP PRAYER & FAST

During what would normally be a mealtime, share together the commitments that you made during the 5 Stops, then pray together — committing each one to God.

YOUR DREAMS

YOUR "LIFE SENTENCE"

YOUR GOALS

REFLECTING
A Look Forward

> **Trust in the LORD with all your heart and lean not on your own understanding; in all your ways acknowledge him, and he will make your paths straight.**
> **Proverbs 3:5-6 (NIV)**

Do you ever wish you could look into the future and see how your life will turn out, what you will become, and what you will accomplish? Probably everyone wishes that at some time in life. God can see the future as clearly as you can see yesterday, but He does not tell everything He knows. He lets us make choices, learn from mistakes, and grow day by day in our relationship with Him so that someday we can look back on our life and see how our choices made a difference.

What choices do you need to make that will make a difference in your future? Are there areas where you need growth? Dreams that you need to pray about? A reputation that you need to work on? Plan and goals to set? This next session is devoted to these areas.

You will make choices about:

1. Your Dreams

2. Your "Life Sentence"

3. Your Goals

MY DREAM LIST

Write in the spaces provided some special dreams that you have for your life in the years to come. Don't write only what you think **will** happen, but dream of what you would **like to happen**. Pray as you are doing this that God will confirm ones He is dreaming with you!

Look back over the dreams you have written and prayed about. To which of these dreams might the Holy Spirit be saying "yes"? Circle the dreams you believe He might want to fulfill in your life.

MY LIFE SENTENCE

Look at your life "backwards" by imagining yourself at the end of your life looking back at the life you lived. What would you like your tombstone to read ... or how do you want people to remember you? Write your "life sentence," or epitaph, on the "tombstone" below.

FOOTPRINTS

One night a man had a dream. He dreamed he was walking along the beach with the Lord. Across the sky flashed scenes from his life. For each scene, he noticed two sets of footprints in the sand; one belonged to him, and the other to the Lord.

When the last scene of his life flashed before him, he looked back at the footprints in the sand. He noticed that many times along the path of his life there was only one set of footprints. He also noticed that it happened at the very lowest and saddest times in his life.

This really bothered him and he questioned the Lord about it. "Lord, you said that once I decided to follow you, you'd walk with me all the way. But I have noticed that during the most troublesome times in my life, there is only one set of footprints. I don't understand why when I needed you most you would leave me."

The Lord replied, "My precious, precious child, I love you and I would never leave you. During your times of trial and suffering, when you see only one set of footprints, it was then that I carried you."

— Anonymous

KEEPING THE FAITH

> **The LORD** himself goes before you and will be with you; he will never leave you nor forsake you. Do not be afraid; do not be discouraged."
>
> Deuteronomy 31:8

Sometimes when you are traveling through life and everything seems fine, suddenly you may experience hindrances and roadblocks that seem to pull your attention away from God. These roadblocks may include temptations, discouragement, hurts, physical ailments, and many others. It is in these times it is very important for you to have reminders that God is with you and He will NEVER leave you alone.

During this retreat you may make many decisions for God, and you will undoubtedly need to have a reminder of this special time with God. Then, during tough times, you can look at that reminder and think of how God worked in your life as a result of the decisions you made this weekend. You can remember the special time spent with Him, when you felt very near to Him, and remember that He is **always** near.

So what will your reminder be? Maybe you would like to go to the place where you took your walk and gather a reminder, such as a leaf representing how you "turned over a new leaf" or a rock to remind you of the stepping-stones that you have experienced this weekend. You may prefer to gather a reminder from another place you have been during the retreat. You can also create your own bookmark or drawing to serve as your reminder! If all else fails and you can't think of **anything**, you could cut out the picture on the bottom of this page as your reminder.

Go now and gather the reminder that you will use to keep you going after this retreat!

>...let us throw off everything that hinders and the sin that so easily entangles, and let us run with perseverance the race marked out for us
>
> Hebrews 12:1

In all thy ways

"Setting Your

	WORSHIP Time Alone With God	RELATIONSHIP Socially	DISCIPLESHIP Accountability
1 - 3 months			
1 year			
2 - 3 years			

... And he shall

acknowledge Him . . .

"Goals With God."

	STEWARDSHIP Time, Talent, Tithe	PARTNERSHIP With God	LEADERSHIP Responsibility
1 - 3 months			
1 year			
2 - 3 years			

direct thy paths Proverbs 3:5-6.

GROUP REJOICING
Sharing "life sentences," prayers, and affirmations.

GROUP REJOICING
Prayer List

NAME	KEEPSAKE	NEED	ANSWERED

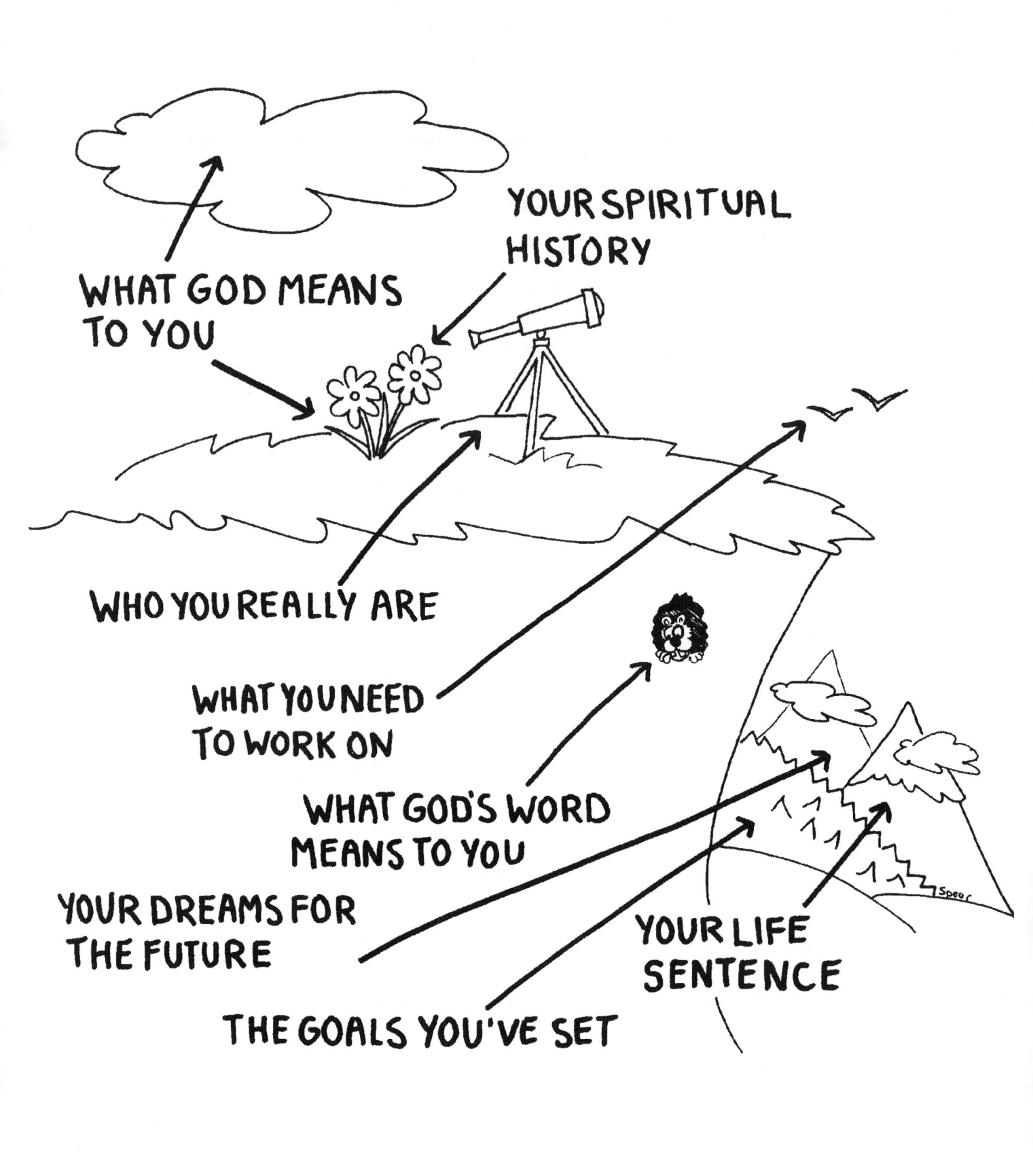

- WHAT GOD MEANS TO YOU
- YOUR SPIRITUAL HISTORY
- WHO YOU REALLY ARE
- WHAT YOU NEED TO WORK ON
- WHAT GOD'S WORD MEANS TO YOU
- YOUR DREAMS FOR THE FUTURE
- YOUR LIFE SENTENCE
- THE GOALS YOU'VE SET

RENEWING...
A New Outlook

During this Weekend Alone With God you have taken a journey through your life with God. Now you are coming to the last leg of that journey, when you will have to go back into your everyday life and live out the commitments you have made during these quiet moments alone with God. But before you take that first step back into your world, take some time to really think about the decisions you have made. Think about:

1. YOUR SPIRITUAL HISTORY

2. WHAT GOD MEANS TO YOU

3. WHO YOU REALLY ARE

4. WHAT YOU NEED TO WORK ON

5. WHAT GOD'S WORD MEANS TO YOU

6. YOUR DREAMS FOR THE FUTURE

7. YOUR LIFE SENTENCE

8. THE GOALS YOU'VE SET

If it seems overwhelming, take heart! All you need is a new perspective. You see, the changes you decide to make and the goals you set are not made to earn God's love - you are already totally loved and accepted by Him! The commitments you make to Him are simply an expression of your love for Him. Because God wants to have a close relationship with you, the most important thing you can do is learn to love Him more and more. Then all the things you need to work on will be easier to do because they are motivated by love for God, not just obligation to Him.

The following pages provide opportunities to enjoy His presence and to express love and gratitude back to Him through prayer and communion.

Prayer of St. Francis of Assisi

Lord,
Make me an instrument of your peace;
Where there is hatred, let me sow love;
Where there is injury, pardon;
Where is doubt, faith;
Where there is despair, hope;
Where there is darkness, light;
Where there is sadness, joy.

O Divine Master,
Grant that I may not so much
seek to be consoled as to console;
To be understood as to understand;
To be loved as to love.

For it is in giving that we receive.
It is in pardoning that we are pardoned.
It is in dying that we
are born to eternal life.

Praying the Lord's Prayer

This weekend retreat has provided many opportunities to talk to God, write to Him, think about Him, find out who He wants you to be, and discover some things that He may want you to do in the future. Now you will have the opportunity to follow the example Christ gave as a model of how we are to pray — "The Lord's Prayer." Write out your own personalized prayer using The Lord's Prayer (found in Matthew 6:9-13) as your model.

Our Father in heaven,
(Identify with God as your personal Father)

Hallowed be your name
(Recognize Him as holy and worthy of honor and reverence)

Your kingdom come, your will be done on earth as it is in heaven.
(Submit to His will and His timing in all areas of life)

Give us today our daily bread.
(Trust Him to provide for your every need)

The Lord's Prayer
(continued)

Forgive us our debts, as we also have forgiven our debtors.
(Confess to Him, receive His forgiveness, and grant forgiveness to others)

And lead us not into temptation, but deliver us from the evil one.
(Ask for His protection and for power over temptation)

For yours is the kingdom and the power and the glory forever. Amen
(End by praising and glorifying God for being so great!)

GROUP REJOICING

THE LORD'S SUPPER

> The Lord Jesus, on the night he was betrayed, took bread, and when he had given thanks, he broke it and said, "This is my body, which is for you; do this in remembrance of me." In the same way, after supper he took the cup, saying, " This cup is the new covenant in my blood; do this, whenever you drink it, in remembrance of me." For whenever you eat this bread and drink this cup, you proclaim the Lord's death until he comes.
>
> 1 Corinthians 11:23-26

What is the significance of the symbols (bread and wine)? These communion elements are visual reminders which serve as :

1. A Memorial to Jesus Christ

2. A Thanksgiving to God

3. A Covenant with Jesus

4. A Fellowship with Jesus

5. A Source of Spiritual Strength

6. A Reminder of our Atonement Through Christ

7. A Declaration of our Eternal Life Through Christ

Let this time of renewal serve as a "seal" upon the commitments you have made this weekend and to rejoice in the love and forgiveness of Jesus.

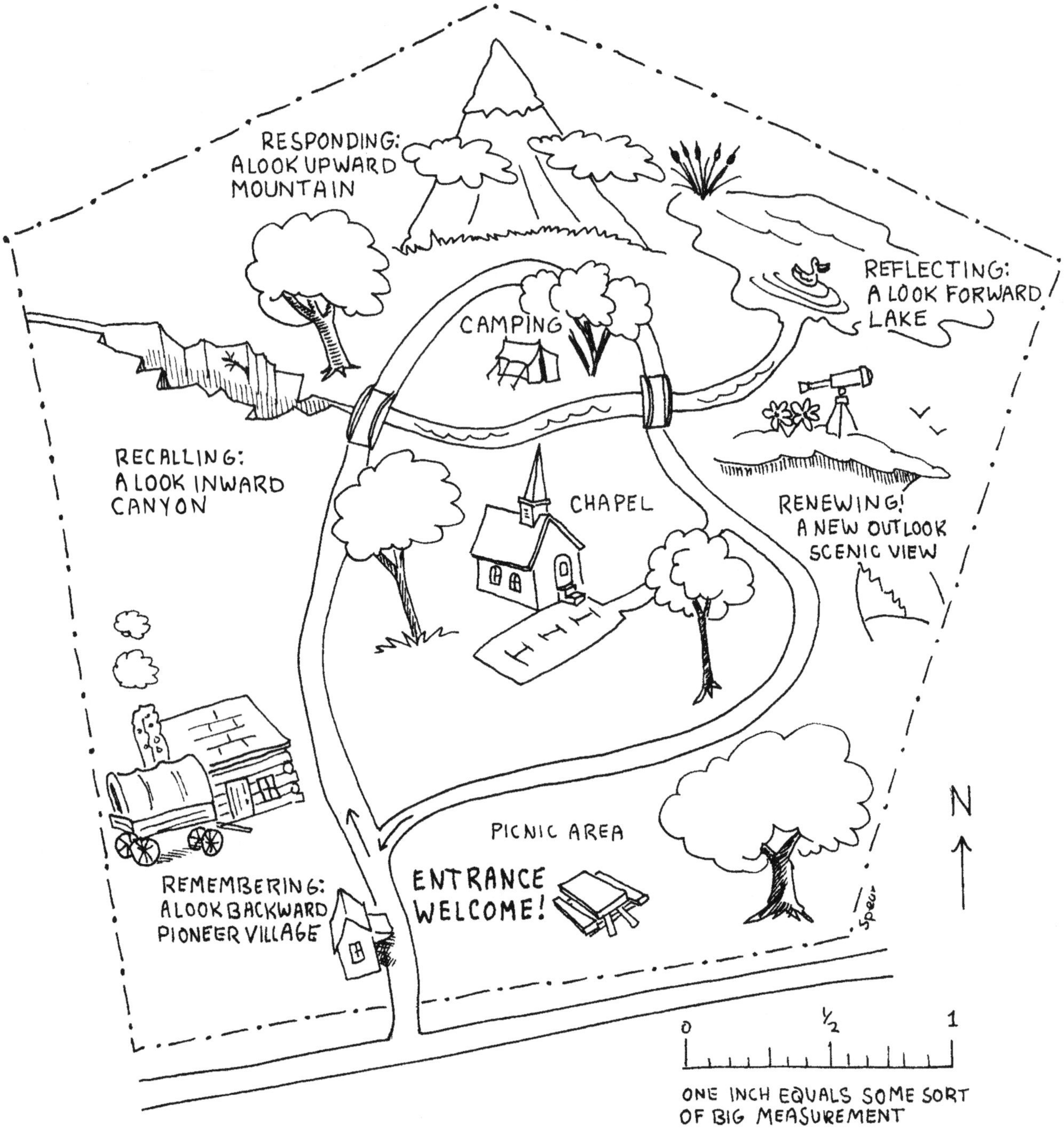
RESPONDING:
A LOOK UPWARD
MOUNTAIN
REFLECTING:
A LOOK FORWARD
LAKE
CAMPING
RECALLING:
A LOOK INWARD
CANYON
CHAPEL
RENEWING!
A NEW OUTLOOK
SCENIC VIEW
N
PICNIC AREA
REMEMBERING:
A LOOK BACKWARD
PIONEER VILLAGE
ENTRANCE
WELCOME!
Spear
0
1/2
1
ONE INCH EQUALS SOME SORT
OF BIG MEASUREMENT

MY RETREAT MAP

Draw below a picture, or map, of the spiritual "journey" you have taken this weekend, showing the points of rest, of change in direction, of decision-making, and whatever else you experienced.

NEXT STEPS FOR GROWTH

DEVOTIONAL NOTES

Youth Resources

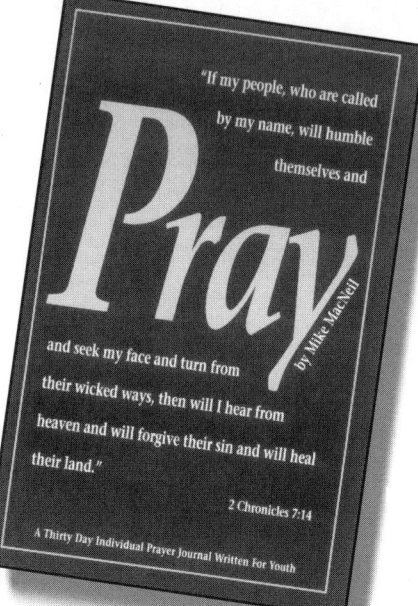

Sharing My Faith — A Teen's Guide To Evangelism
edited by Mark Gilroy
Designed to help teens overcome the questions and fears they have about witnessing. This book shows the right time to witness, how to naturally bring up spiritual matters and more.
BKQ48 **$5.95**

Thirty to One
by Phil Stevenson
This book is a practical guide to personal holiness and mission. It leads you through thirty days of personal growth culminating in a day away with God.
HA283 **$6.95**

Pray
by Mike MacNeil
A thirty day prayer journal written for youth. Includes Scripture verses, life applications, suggestions for using prayer in your daily life, and charts for prayer requests and answers.
BKH41 **$3.95**

To Place Your Order Call:
Wesleyan Publishing House ♦ 800-493-7539 (800-4 WESLEY)